Donald Macintyre

On the Antiquity of the Gaelic Language Shewing its Affinity

to Hebrew, Greek and Latin

Superseding the Masoretic Points and Furnishing a Key to the Hebrew

Vowel Sounds

Donald Macintyre

On the Antiquity of the Gaelic Language Shewing its Affinity to Hebrew, Greek and Latin
Superseding the Masoretic Points and Furnishing a Key to the Hebrew Vowel Sounds

ISBN/EAN: 9783337417789

Printed in Europe, USA, Canada, Australia, Japan

Cover: Foto ©Thomas Meinert / pixelio.de

More available books at **www.hansebooks.com**

ON THE

ANTIQUITY OF THE GAELIC LANGUAGE

SHEWING ITS

AFFINITY TO HEBREW, GREEK, AND LATIN,

SUPERSEDING THE MASORETIC POINTS,

AND

FURNISHING A KEY TO THE HEBREW VOWEL SOUNDS:

An Essay.

BY THE REV. D. M'INTYRE,

MINISTER OF KINCARDINE.

EDINBURGH:

MACLACHLAN AND STEWART, 64 SOUTH BRIDGE.
LONDON: SIMPKIN, MARSHALL, & CO.

MDCCCLXV.

PREFACE.

THE progress hitherto made to give the Gaelic language its legitimate rank among early European tongues appears to me unsatisfactory. I have devoted the following pages to that subject, and hope it may be found a step in the proper direction. I feel impelled, by a sense of duty, to make public the marked sameness, in vowel sounds, I have lately detected between the Gaelic and the Hebrew. That was my chief object in writing the Essay; and I trust the evidence adduced throughout is sufficiently cogent to show at once, that the sacred original of the Old Testament can be best read and understood by means of its own textual vowels, safe from the smallest risk of error, without calling in the aid of the fanciful system of Rabbinical points.

D. M'INTYRE.

KINCARDINE MANSE, *March* 1865.

ANTIQUITY OF THE GAELIC LANGUAGE.

THE grammar of the Gaelic is already written and its diction-
ary compiled. The object of the following paper is to trace
up the language in its connection with other early Eastern
tongues, so as to assign to it the place among them which it
unquestionably claims. The simple and expressive form it
presents in its construction, abounding in simple monosyllabic
roots—all conveying a primitive expression of ideas, separately
taken up as they occur in our ordinary intercourse with surround-
ing objects and things—assigns to it an early Eastern origin.
These simple independent elements of speech are again found
welded together in two or more members, to give expression
to complex ideas; and by the further embellishment of affixes,
made available for communicating all thought, in the full
luxuriance of elegant diction. No language that we happen to be
acquainted with, ancient or modern, is more remarkable in this
respect than the Gaelic. By the means just stated, it is found
to communicate, in expressive form, the entire creation of the
fancy in its various regions. It combines, complexes, simpli-
fies, separates, our notions of all objects presented to our senses,
in the exact relation in which they stand to one another and
to us. This quality the Gaelic has derived from being, time
out of mind, more a spoken than a written language. Its tone,
and idiom, and accent, are preserved pure and entire, free from
the damaging influence of foreign intermixture. A written
language, from misspelling and mistonation, not to insist on
other causes, is much more liable to change—call it improvement if you will—than a spoken one. That appears to us to
account for the high preservation, in tone and accent, which
the Gaelic presents. Nothing short of a complete knowledge
of it, as a spoken tongue, will be convincive of the fact.

It is greatly to be regretted that philologists dealing with the subject have hitherto been unsuccessful in so tracing up to its origin this fine old language, as to assign to it its legitimate place among the early vehicles of human intercourse. The latest attempt in that direction that has been made is scarcely more successful than its predecessors : I allude to the pamphlet by Professor Blackie of Edinburgh, on the Gaelic language, published in November last. The style and taste of this production is, to say the least of it, somewhat peculiar. We do not feel disposed to be offended, considering that the style is peculiar to the writer—more so, perhaps, than his casket of complimentary adjectives applies to us in these parts. The laudations and the censures of this amusing lecturer, as they are alternately poured out so freely upon our heads, as Highlanders, will neither elate us, nor disturb our equanimity. We are much more thin-skinned on the question of his philological inaccuracies, which shall be adverted to at the proper point, than we are when he touches our nationality and language in this *ex officio* fashion. Whatever we are in these respects, we take other weapons than those wielded by the Professor, to stand our ground and defend ourselves. We do not doubt that he knows Greek well, but we know Gaelic better,—we know it as our mother tongue—our first language, in all the native peculiarity of its structure, idiom, and accent. We learn no Gaelic from Professor Blackie, and shall not with impunity allow him, or any other Scot or Saxon, to give a more subordinate place to our beautiful language than that which legitimate philology assigns to it. But I must proceed now to lay this before the inspection of the intelligent reader. It is needless to try to convince those who allow a mixtion of prejudice and partiality to block up the channel of their belief, or, failing better means, resort to the artifice of browbeating, to drive their dupes into their own way of thinking. It is needless, I repeat, to try to convince these ; and in this essay I have not such beings in my eye, nor can I hope to convince them. I let them alone.

In tracing up the affinity of the Gaelic with the Hebrew, the first thing to be done is to brush out the Rabbinical points from among the sacred text. Until that is done, or at any rate, until they are entirely ignored, which is the same thing, let no one be so foolish as to look for success. No individual, possessing any tolerable acquaintance with the subject, needs be astonished at the fruitless attempts of those who try their skill at the task by means of a pointed Hebrew lexicon.

It will be necessary here briefly to touch upon the principal arguments for and against the use of the Masoretic points, as they are called, which agitated the Biblical schools of Europe for more than two hundred years; and then show how the Gaelic, by its affinity with the Hebrew, settles at once that much vexed question. Did Louis Cappellus, the great anti-punctist champion, possess a knowledge of the Gaelic, and did he apply it, he could by that means alone cut away every inch of ground from under his opponents; but neither he nor any other of those who engaged in that controversy knew anything, so far as we ever heard, of that language. There are three opinions put forward on the subject of these points, and very keenly contested, from opposite points of view, by the disputants in that Biblical controversy.

I. The opinion of the two Buxtorffs—the father and son—and in consideration of their respectable scholarship, drew to their side not a few eminent names, who hold that the Masoretic points, by means of which the Hebrew should be pronounced, were at first invented by Ezra, and consequently of the same Divine authority with the consonants.

II. The opinion of those who deny the Divine authority of these vowel points, and maintain that they were invented by the Masorets or Doctors of the School of Tiberias, five hundred years after the time of our Saviour. This opinion was first announced by Rabbi Elias Levita, in the beginning of the sixteenth century, and adopted by Louis Cappellus, a Protestant Divine of the French Church, and Professor of Hebrew in the University of Saumur. It was also adopted by many great men, among whom were Calvin, Luther, Scaliger, Masclef and others; and by Bishops Walton, Hare, and Lowth, Drs Kennicot and Geddes.

III. A third opinion was advanced by Dr Prideaux, who steers a middle course between the other two, and attempts to maintain that the points were invented earlier than the fifth century of the Christian era, and soon after Ezra's time. It is by a line of special pleading he endeavours to do this, with the formidable evidences of probability and presumption against him. He ventures to maintain that the points *might* have been invented, although not alluded to by divines of the early Christian eras, and that it was necessary they *should* have been invented, so as to preserve from oblivion the proper pronunciation of the language. With regard to this opinion, it is humbly thought, with due deference to Dr Prideaux, that if the points existed, and had to fulfil the important office he ascribes to them, they *would* most certainly be mentioned by the writers of these times, and by the Christian Fathers; and it is perfect folly to say that they preserve entire the original pronunciation of the Hebrew, which could not be preserved in its integrity as late as Ezra's time, nor after the captivity.

Let me now briefly go over the chief arguments in the other two opinions, and in their order.

I. The arguments in support of the Buxtorff theory are seemingly more plausible than those advanced by Prideaux; and even they are brought to the ground by Cappellus and his followers. One is that the books Zohar and Bahir, said to have been written about our Saviour's time, make mention of the Hebrew points as then existing. On examination, however, these books are proved to contain unmistakable evidence, external and internal, of an origin at least one thousand years later, and they contain, as a whole, nothing that is interesting or valuable, but a mass of Rabbinical rubbish of their time. The only other argument necessary to be mentioned, as put forward by the punctists, is that our Saviour is supposed to have alluded to the Hebrew points, being part of the law, by the expression " one jot or one title," in Matt. v. 18. If this could be substantiated, it would of itself be supreme, but when examined it falls to the ground. The Greek words ιοτα and κεραια, rendered in our version " jot and title," unquestionably mean the Hebrew yod ׳ its smallest letter, and κεραια, from the root κερας, a small horn or beak of a letter, attached to it and part of it, and not a detached point, as Buxtorff would have it. Besides, we may mention, by the way, that κερας is derived from the Celtic root céir, a beak or scallop, hence ceireanach, having a scallopy outline. So this adventurous argument for the points turns out as futile as its antecedent; and these two being the most cogent and plausible, it would be a waste of time to go over the others.

II. The arguments against the points, and adopted by the great authorities above named, are so conclusive and convincing to any unbiassed mind, that we only need refer to a few of them. And (1.), that the Hebrew, like other languages derived from it, has textual vowels in its own alphabet to regulate its pronunciation. (2.) That according to these, the LXX. version was made about two hundred and eighty-six years before the Christian era, and the Hexaplar of Origen five hundred years later. (3.) That the Masoretic points were not heard of until the middle of the tenth century, as is vouched by the writings of Rabbi Ben Asher and Rabbi Ben Naphtali, respectively chiefs of the Western and Eastern Schools, and who flourished at that period. And (4.) that the scriptures used in the service of the synagogue to this day are without points; so is the copy found by Dr Buchanan in Central India, in the possession of the black Jews, which they must have got at some era from the land of Israel. All these proofs clearly demolish every pretension to the integrity of the Rabbinical points.

Let us now consider how improbable a thing it is, that writers like the Rabbins, so addicted to tradition, and so given to mixing up their own ludicrous marvels with the textual sense of Scripture, can be depended upon in their theory of *sound*, when they are detected so often at fault in their version of the *sense* of the sacred text. We are happily enabled to correct their errors in the latter instance, by consulting the context for ourselves; the only effectual way now to correct them in the former instance is to brush their points totally away, and leave the sacred text to be read and understood, as the Jews of old did, by means of its own textual vowels. I am quite aware that the idea has been abroad for some time back, and gaining ground in our universities of late, that the Hebrew class cannot be properly taught without putting the students to the trouble of learning to read by means of the points.* This notion, we know very well, has been imported into this country from Germany, and not without some danger of a garniture of neology along with it. Those who may be captivated by the merit or marvel of the vowel points and Rabbinical erudition, had better weigh the subject of their admiration a little better. Let me state to them an instance, not a whit more extravagant than a thousand others, of the Rabbinical learning and genius, in accounting for a textual omission. In one of the alphabetical Psalms (cxlv.), the verse or stanza of the letter *nun* י is wanting, in at least some of the copies used by the Rabbins. Such an omission is now ordinarily accounted for as having taken place through the mere *incuria* of the transcriber. The Rabbinical way of accounting for it is characteristic. It is this: David, when composing the Psalm in question, when he came on with his theme as far as the letter י (*nun*), saw a terrible vision,—the dreadful *nephele* mentioned in Isa. xxiv. 20, which begins by the letter *nun;* so he passed over that letter in his fright, and hastened to the next one, the comfortable *samech* ס! From that specimen of the Biblical lore of the authors of the points, let me entreat all punctist readers, including teachers and taught, of the Hebrew Scriptures, seriously to consider the origin of the foundation on which they rest their belief of the genuine mode of interpreting the Word of God. For my own part, I feel compelled to admit that it is nothing short of a species of

* The student who learns Hebrew by the pointed system only, and not by the unpointed mode as well, labours under greater disadvantage than the student who was taught by the latter system. This is it: Put an unpointed Hebrew Bible into the hands of the former, and he cannot make out one sentence of it correctly, or at all; but give the latter a pointed Bible, and, by merely ignoring the Masoretic points, he makes out every word of it.

heterodoxy now to trust the sense of Scripture to these points, or to the views of their fanciful authors. Another absurdity is observable in the plan of pronunciation they have devised. They suppress into what they call quiescent letters the Hebrew textual vowels אהוי, the *matres lectiones* of the ancients, and yet they are compelled to repudiate their own act; for we find these very letters, by the points of these very men, in very many cases, made to give out their proper sounds, by the expedient, forsooth, of a vowel point fixed under or over them. I accordingly ask the admiring successors of the Masorites, how is it that we find, in reading the pointed Hebrew Bible, that א and ה are most commonly pointed by *kametz*, ⊤, or *pathah*, −, or by *tsere*, ⋅⋅, or *scgol*, ∴? Why is the presence of the *yod* י necessary in long *hirck* י? And why is the *shurek* ו never pronounced without the ו? It is because there dwell in these letters these very sounds, virtually and inherently, by the test of all antiquity, which the Rabbins, even in their zeal for the marvellous, tremble to suppress. Their successors should show a similar yielding to what is reasonable and right, and return, in the full belief of it, to the reading of the Hebrew Scriptures as they were originally read. The textual vowels of the language are quite sufficient for the purpose, by proofs cogent and clear already urged, and now by the farther testimony of a living, spoken, ancient, independent language— living and spoken without any material change for the last three thousand years. At this point, then, I introduce the Gaelic language as the living witness of the fact. In doing it I am obliged to say of myself, that it was my first language, from being born, brought up, and educated in the parish of Kilmalie, Lochaber, which may be reckoned central Caledonia, where that language has been spoken in its greatest purity time out of mind, removed from the damaging influences of border intermixture with foreign dialects. When I attended the Divinity Hall I was taught Hebrew with and without points, the latter system in Glasgow and the former in Aberdeen. When in the Glasgow Hebrew class, I remember detecting a striking affinity between Hebrew and Gaelic, and pointing it out to our Professor, the learned Dr Fleming, now Professor of Moral Philosophy. Not knowing anything then of the pointed mode, or the difference in its pronunciation from the system I was acquiring, it did not occur to me to mark the similarity of sound as well as that of sense in words in both languages. Towards the end of the session, I remember our eminent Professor recommending to us, for our own private satisfaction, to know the pointed mode of reading, and to compare the two. In order to accomplish this I next session attended the Aberdeen Divinity Hall, where I also took the Hebrew class, and soon acquired the pointed system. I now knew the difference in pronunciation between the two readings, but even then, and ~~not~~ for more than thirty years after, it did not occur to me that the Gaelic furnished the key by which to see into the region of Hebrew vowel sounds. This I accidentally discovered in the summer of 1862, while one day poring over Hebrew roots, comparing passages with our present Gaelic version of the Scriptures. Since I detected this, in all the search I have made, I have not met a single instance of similarity in sound with the pointed system of pronunciation. That of itself is, to my mind, ample evidence and proof that the entire machinery of Masoretic points, as a phonetic agency, should at once and for ever be discarded.

It will, I think, be conceded by philologists that the Gaelic language is the oldest spoken language in the world. The celebrated Dr Blair says that no considerable progress in philology can be made without it. It has for its vowels *a, e, i, o, u,* corresponding with the Hebrew textual vowels, ו, ע, י, ה, א. By means of these, without any points, the Samaritans read the Bible. The consonants of both languages are similar in the office they fulfil. The aspirates and gutturals very similar. Both languages have but two genders; both do not show a present tense of the verb, and show a marked sameness in the structure of the other tenses, and in both the future is occasionally used for the preterite. Then, all that we have to do is to produce a class of words in the two languages with *vowels* the same, *consonants* the same, *meaning* the same, and syllabic *arrangement* the same. If we can do this we will have three points *mutually conceded* by the Gaelic and Hebrew, and only require to find out the sound of the latter. The Gaelic furnishes the key to us, and here it is,—

האר	גאל	אור	את	אשר	אנש	אנה	*Hebrew.*
taruin	gabhail	asair	ad	asri'	ainis	anech	*Gaelic.*
draw	recover	trapping	this or that	procedure	desti- tute	gasping or moaning	

We have here the sound of א revived and the same as that of *a* in Gaelic. I must observe that the slight variation in the Gaelic spelling is in consequence of the standing rule, "broad to broad, and small to small," which must uniformly be observed. I have to point out that a selection is made of Hebrew words whose first letter is a vowel, in case it might be thought that a precedent consonant might in any way tend to damp or to stifle the free native sound of the vowel. I have also furnished instances of the vowel the second letter of the root, and the result is precisely the same. I make no doubt, however, that semitones of all the vowels may be discovered by farther research.

Take now a class of words to make out the sound of ה agreeing with è.

מהר	זה	בלה	כה	הוא		הל	ה	*Hebrew.*
mear	sè	bleth	bao	è bha		ealamh	è	*Gaelic.*
hastily	this	to wear	void	was		quick	this or that	

The sound and spelling in these, as in the former class, are substantially the same, with a slight evidence of the semitone in some cases.

Take next a class of words with the י as the first letter.

שכינ	ימש	יש	יאת	ינה	יאל	ילל	יאמר	*Hebrew.*
sgian	amis	es	iat	inne	àil ial	illail	iamra	*Gaelic.*
knife	feel	he, it	agree	squeeze	will	yelling	mention	

The next Hebrew vowel ע, the sound of *o*, is the same in form as the old Runic ᚨ, the only difference is that the latter is inverted and the same in sound. I mention this because the ע has been the subject of some controversy, since it is a radical letter, the other vowels being all serviles. That it agrees with the Gaelic *o* is unquestionable.

רעל	קער	נער	בעה	מער	עלע	עבר	*Hebrew.*
rola	còr	naor	bogha	mòd	òl	obeir	*Gaelic.*
a roll	large	a child	bulge	a meeting	swallow	work, a servant	

The semitone in two at least of the above words in the sound of *o* is observable. Under ו we have

דוה	זוה	מול	מור	ולד	וזר	*Hebrew.*
dubhach	suidhe	mul	tùr	ulidh	useir	*Gaelic.*
sickly	incline	boundary	mountain	child	burden	

We have to add to the foregoing evidence of identity a still more interesting class of words, such as have been written to save space and time, without any of the textual vowels. This is a numerous class, and have been put forward by punctists as one of the strong points of their system, to require the aid of vowel points to pronounce them. It is, however, but a species of stenography common to all languages; and were we in any doubt of what vowels to call to our aid in pronouncing these words, the Gaelic furnishes a directory. In the majority of cases, it is the short sound of א for the first syllable, and that of ה in the second as a general rule, that seems to be required. Thus—

כר	תבנ	שפר	ששה	שק	פקר	רבר	נחל	Hebrew.
cár	taban	saibhir	seisear	sác	faicid	dabair	gathail	Gaelic.
curve	handful	rich	six	sack	visit	saying	flame	

After this array of evidence of the natural sounds of the five vowels, and how to deal with words without them, evincing in the aggregate the strong marks of affinity of Gaelic and Hebrew, it will scarcely do for Professor Blackie to hazard the assertion of pages 7, 8, of his pamphlet, to the contrary. If he finds himself misled, we leave him to settle the difference with his Gesenius as he best may. We cannot allow his assertion to go forth as fact in the face of this overwhelming testimony against its accuracy. He is evidently not at home with Celtic philology, into which he dabbles, and had better avoid jumping into hasty conclusions regarding it.

Still farther to satisfy the fastidious credibility of such critics as may hesitate their condescendence, I beg to refer them to the testimony of antiquity in support of the evidence already adduced. As far back as the second and third centuries, the Christian Fathers, in their writings, supply us with ample proofs of the mode then of pronouncing the Hebrew. St Jerome, the most eminent of the Latin Fathers, and who wrote in the fourth century very valuable works on the Scriptures, assures us of the mode of reading Hebrew by the divines of the second and third centuries. Neither he nor any other Christian writer of his time makes any mention or any allusion to vowel points. He produces extracts from the Hexaplar of Origen, by far the most valuable Biblical relic of antiquity, in which we have shown to us, by means of Greek characters, the very sounds and intonations by which the Hebrew was then read, and we shall see how very nearly it agrees to what the Gaelic makes it. Accordingly, the first verse of the 11th chapter of Hosea—

קראתי	וממצרים	והבהו	ישראל	נער	כי	Hebrew.
καραθι	ουμεμεσραιμ	ουεαδνου	Ισραηλ	νερ	χι	{ Hebrew in Greek characters.

We might give further extracts were it necessary. It will not do for us to treat these testimonies lightly. We will be left without excuse if we do, for intermeddling with a subject at once solemn and important in its reference to us. This testimony has been handed down to our times, from remote ages, along with the sacred record which is to be at all times the ground of our faith and the rule of our lives. The tones of any language are an essential part of it which should, in our mouths, be preserved in its greatest purity, and not allowed, by the caprice of individual taste, to be marred or changed. The tones of the sacred original of the Bible should by all means be continued unchanged, as its vowels and consonants are, and will be, unchanged throughout the whole chapter of time.

It is inexpedient, we humbly submit, for the Biblical scholars of this country to repair to the schools of the Continent, where strange sounds may be the chief thing they have to acquire. To the course of the Rhine and the Elbe they may go to acquire, as they think, the right Hebrew sounds, but they all the while leave at their elbow at home, unheeded and unobserved, a venerable tongue to guide their path much nearer that point than anything in Germany can do. They should first acquire the spoken languages of their own country, two only in number, and then they would be in a position of forming a right estimate of home produce, and its value to them, ere they import from foreign countries any manufacture unsuitable to the temper and literary taste of our climate. It may be thought a fine thing to give fanciful sounds to words, as if that were to improve the sense. So the Germans and their admirers think proper, as they imagine, to improve the tones of the Hebrew text by a system of points. The wonder is, that the scholastic vein of this country should not practise that art in softening down the high pitches of their good native English. Let us see how it would do. Take any two or three words, say—

man,   day,   house;

garnish them by one set of Masoretic points, and you have—

moon,   doah,   hash;

or with another, and you change them into—

min,   du,   hess.

But is that any improvement upon man, day, house? Not a whit more rational is the Masoretic system of Hebrew punctuation. With respect to the above quotation from the Hexaplar, let me finally remark, that the א, the י, and the ו have invariably the Gaelic sounds of the corresponding vowels *a*, *i*, *u*; the ה has sometimes the short sound of *e*, sometimes the long one of *è*; and the ע seems to have the sound of *e*, or *āō*, as in נער, the Gaelic *naor*. These slight variations from the original rule no doubt came to be practised after the captivity, leaning as it does to the Chaldaic dialect, which was incorporated at that period with the Hebrew. The only other remark I have to make on this part of the subject of this essay is, that the only use which the Masoretic points may subserve, is merely to shew, as a sort of glossary, the parts of the verb, cases of nouns, and the like, as the Rabbins understood it in their day, but never to be accepted as a vehicle of sound.

To aid us in arriving at that conclusion, we shall now proceed to examine what countenance is received by the affinity existing between the Gaelic or Celtic and the Greek and Latin languages. I have bestowed some attention on this subject already; and, by the courtesy of the editor of the "Inverness Courier" have, in an article in the literary columns of that paper, shown evidences of close affinity between the three languages in question. All that I require to do here is to exhibit the same proof in a more extended form. Accordingly, let any one who is fond of such studies take up a Greek Lexicon, run his finger along the order of the alphabet, and he will meet with Celtic roots in scores and dozens. He must be warned that he will find many of them welded into other words, or parts of words, to fit in with what Horace calls the *ore rotundo Graiis*, by intonation and accent, to become tolerable to Grecian enunciation. In this way the edges and corners of the Celtic roots are considerably rubbed off. Others however are, and in great numbers, in their purely Celtic forms, exhibited with the Greek affix attached to make them available to the vocabulary of that language. With a class of these, of similar spelling and meaning in Greek and Gaelic, we shall presently deal. It is to be observed in the outset that *a* privative is common to the two languages, the negative particles, intensive prefixes, and nouns, verbs, &c., such as—

Gaelic,	athar	an	fear	amar	anam	ăr	bean	bò
Greek,	αιθερ	αν	ανερ	αμαρα	ανεμος	αροω	εανα	βους

Gaelic,	bras	bus	bè	gean	gin	garbh	gnu	dia	&c.
Greek,	βραβια	βυσμα	βη	γανος	γινομαι	γραφω	γρυζω	διος	

These and many more less distinct meet us before going over four letters of the alphabet. It is unnecessary to produce more examples. Let me point out here to Professor Blackie and other Grecians, that in the above list we have in every case the Celtic the root, and in every case the Greek the derivative. The primitive trunk or body of the word is pure Celtic, and by an affix, or prefix, or increment superinduced, it becomes Grecian. There is no use trying to ignore that fact. The trunk or root without the affix is fully intelligible; the affix by itself is a meaningless babble. Grecians have had the loan of our Celtic roots now for some thousands of years in the building up of their language; and if they cannot do without the loan, let them at least acknowledge it. If they demur to this, let them lop off their graft and be away with it; our Celtic root remains to us undamaged and undestroyed in the full power of its original meaning, as it was before receiving this same Grecian graft. In the Gaelic we never meet Greek roots with Celtic affixes. This will surely show which of these languages claims the higher antiquity. But to make it clear in another form, let us take one of the above words and submit it to a legitimate analysis—take the verb γραφω, lop off the ω, and it becomes γραφ—meaningless in Greek. We recognise it now as the same with *garbh*, which means rough, and is thus reconciled. In primitive times, it is well known that the ground on which the ancients wrote was first smoothened by a film of gummy substance. The letters were then scratched or engraved by the stilum into that surface, which roughened it all over; the written surface was then *garbh*, roughened or scratched, as we shall show by and by to have been the import of the Latin verb *scribo*. Now γραφ or *garbh* is derived from *gar*, roughness, which shows a regular family of derivatives, such as *garach*, *garrachan, garblach, garbhadh, garbhan,* &c. These are formed by assuming the pertinent affixes, which the Gaelic so profusely supplies for accommodating every additional phase of significancy. A similar result can be arrived at by analysing any of the others. From hence we arrive at this conclusion. (1.) That the Gaelic forms a large element in the primitive groundwork of the Greek; (2.) That the Gaelic, being a living language, revives the proper pronunciation of Greek; and (3.) That we in Scotland have in this respect the advantage of our neighbours to the south of the Tweed. The somewhat intricate sound of it, the η, is brought down to us by the ϛη, the bleat of the sheep, which has not changed in tone any more than the song of the lark. Professor Blackie may dignify us for this by complimentary appellatives from his choice casket, such as "Semito-Celtic visionaries," "British boobies—people without a soul," and the like; which, if I am to understand as an attempt at browbeating, I can only pity as a pointless effort. I would be much more willing to accept the whole tirade as a sort of harmless, funny bravado, meaning to convey no ill-will, but merely a passing squib for the amusement of his tyro listeners.

I now proceed to exhibit a comparison between the Gaelic and the Latin. Similar observations will apply here as in the last case; the affinity is even more striking and extensive. This was naturally to be expected, from the juxtaposition of Latium to Gaul, and the long space of time these languages, or rather the tribes speaking them, possessed these conterminous provinces. It will be superfluous to produce a long list of corresponding roots, they meet us in dozens in every page. Take the following,

Gaelic,	a	as	anam	arm	ăr	balbh	băt
Latin,	a	abs	anima	arma	aro	balbus	bates
Gaelic,	can	cèir	dùr	each	scriobh	saighid	&c.
Latin,	cano	cera	durus	equus	scribo	sagittus	

It is equally remarkable here, as in Greek, that the root is Celtic, the affix Latin. The close affinity of Greek and Latin shows itself in the striking similarity of their terminations. Lop away the Latin affix, and the Celtic stock sustains no damage. It stands out in bold relief and full significance, only vastly improved by the work of the pruning-knife. It has sufficient power of its own, and abundant resource to throw out branches, to become the ornamental linguistic tree among its early kindred tongues. It is neither beauty nor fashion to it to have received the graft from Latium, or become the stock upon which stood so many blooming standards in their fruitful and flourishing orchard. The amusing part of it is, that a large class of shallow scholastics, but who plume themselves on their knowledge in classic lore, while they actually don't know the rudiments of the science, set out arrogantly to ignore, if not wholly cast aside, the claims of the language to its legitimate rank of antiquity, which supplies to both Greek and Latin so much of their first foundation, and beauty, and significance. Take away these Celtic stones and Celtic cement, and you leave those tongues of boasted beauty, a perforated, crazy, unsightly ruin. But I must show that now, with reference to the Latin. From the foregoing class of words, let us analyse one or two of ancient and extensive usage in the two languages. Take *arma*, a primitive noun, as Latinists think, signifying weapons of war. Lop off the affix *a*, and you leave it *arm*, a word which a Latinist cannot recognise in his language. A Celt knows it at once, and signifies arms or weapons of war. He knows farther that it is a compound of *àr*, slaughter, and *uidheam*, pronounced *uim*, implements; *ar-uim* contracted *arm*, a weapon or weapons of war. By this analysis, which we know to be right, we at once see the comparative claim to antiquity of the Gaelic and the Latin. Let this not be decided on a solitary instance, take one or two cases more. *Sagittarius*, a Latinist knows to mean bowman, and derived from *sagittus*, an arrow; beyond that he cannot trace it. *Sagittar* without the *ius* he does not know; but a Celt does, and knows it to be compounded of *saighid* and *fear*, an arrowsman. This is not all. He knows *saighid* to be made up of the two words *sath*, to thrust, and *it*, feather, that is, a thrusting feather. The arrow of the ancients had an eagle's feather fixed in the butt-end for the steerage of the weapon. Take now *scribo*, the verb to write, take off the affix *o* and it becomes *scrib*, a word not to be found in the entire Latin vocabulary. However, *scrib* or *scriob* is a Celtic word, meaning a stroke or scar; but *scriob* is a compound of *scàr*, a scratch, and *guib* (genitive of *gob*), a bill-pointed instrument—that is, *scàr-guib*, contracted *scriob*, writing—or the work done by the *stilum* or other pen used in writing by the ancients. The express meaning of these compounds, when taken down and shown in their primitive state, assures us that our analysis is legitimate and right. We at once reject, as effete and impertinent, any analysis that fails to show that. I must here express my profound surprise and disappointment at Professor Blackie giving out, at page 26 of his pamphlet, that the Gaelic *scriob* is derived from the Latin *scribo!* This only equals in peculiarity that *Eaglais* (*eug-lios*, cemetery) is from *Ecclesia*, and *relic* (*rè-lac*, a grave) from *reliqua*, a relic! The Greek verb ἐκκαλέω, which means, to call together or to assemble, is from the Celtic root *glaodh*. That doctrine is as extravagant as to assert that the Greek has been wandering all over Wales, and Ireland, and the Highlands of Scotland (p. 1)! If it has, where has it left a single trace of its existence? Nowhere, is our answer; except perhaps in the amusing conception of those who would arrogate to it, however unjustly, a priority of claim to antiquity over the language which, as we have seen, supplies to it so largely its ground-plan and structure. For the life of me, I cannot make out what the averment means, unless indeed it may be this, that wherever the Professor plants his foot during his summer rambles, it gives the ground the impress of ancient Grecian soil; but we take leave to assure him that neither the tread of his foot, nor the dash of his pen, will have that transforming power, any more than the shake of his hand could convert a "Celtic boatman in lively Oban, or a Celtic shepherd in desolate Sutherland (p. 3)," into an accomplished Hellenist. With evidence so convincing before us, as we have adduced, which is a mere fraction to what can be added, if that were thought necessary, of the superior claim to antiquity possessed by the Gaelic over Greek and Latin, and other members of the Japhetic class, it would be equally unnatural to try to argue it down, as it would be in a stone-mason to argue, with all the stolid fixity of his genius, the same high antiquity to any old wall as to the quarry from which the building materials were excavated. It would betray a want of belief of what is apparent and real to insist on more evidence. If once apparent and undoubted, what more is required? One convincing proof is as good as a hundred. If one is rejected, why not the hundred? The greatest discoveries have been made on small solitary glimpses of evidence. The finest problem in Astronomy had its basis on the small parallaxal angle of the transit of Venus; yet by those few seconds the distance of the sun was computed. The law of gravitation was suggested by the fall of an apple from a tree, and the steam-engine from the boiling bubbles of a tea-kettle.

It would be interesting, at the point we have come to, if we could by legitimate means mark the era at which the tribes, afterwards called Celts, left Canaan for the west. From Upper Canaan they must have made their exit, from the number of pure Hebrew words they retained in their language. There is no other cause that could account for that fact except a migration from the Hebrew country, when the language was spoken and written in its greatest purity. We have no account that the Celtic tribes ever again returned to Canaan once they fairly set face westward. In their progress in that direction, and intercommunion with tribes speaking other languages or dialects, whether on the banks of the Araxis or otherwhere in ancient Scythia, it was that the Celtic entered as an element in the foundation of the Greek language. A similar process brought it to the province where the Latin was first formed into an independent speech, throughout which we find the Celtic intermixed so freely. Successive waves of Celtic-speaking tribes from the East brought the language to Gaul and to Britain at some prehistoric period difficult now to determine with any certainty. One point seems certain, that the Celts were the aborigines or first settlers of these realms, and with various fortunes, during many centuries, settled themselves at last as the unconquered possessors of ancient Caledonia. To this day their descendants, speaking their language, hold no inconsiderable portion of the old provinces.

Every available channel of civil history has been rummaged with a view to fix the probable era at which the Celts migrated from the East, without any satisfactory result. The researches of Cluverius, Polloutier, Mallet, and others, and Sir William Jones and Mr Pinkerton, would seem to fix that era about the year 1400 A.C. About nine hundred years thereafter they were found in the neighbourhood of the Pyrenees, and in Gaul in the time of Julius Cæsar. We are not informed when they came to the Pyrenees, or when to Gaul. We are still at sea on these points. That the Celts were there for a long period is obvious from the number of compound words of their language we find throughout Julius Cæsar's book, which the Latins took up and incorporated with their own speech. These words, in the hands of proficient Gaelic scholars, are easily divided, down through the proper cleavage plane, into their primitive monosyllabic roots, such as the names of men, *Vergubretus, i.e., fear-gu-breth*, a judge; *Orgetorix, i.e., oighre-tigh-righ*, heir of the royal line, &c. Names of rivers, *Rhodannus, Garumna, Rhenus, Sequana*, that is, *Ruadhamhain, Garbhamhain, Reamhain, Seachd-* or *Seimh-amhain*, meaning respectively *red-river, rough-river, smooth-river*, and *still-river*, or probably *seven-river*, from being formed by the confluence of seven large tributaries.

Might we not now inquire if sacred history will favour the opinion formed by these writers, and founded on their researches? The historical facts recorded in the Bible have the first claim to our belief, and we would at once cast to the winds any human production, ancient or modern, tending to weaken our credibility. It is ascertained from Bible history that famine and war were the chief causes which moved tribes to migrate from one country to another. Should we not from these causes, and their effects, try to detect the era of the westward migration of the Celts? There is a very strong probability that the event happened about seventeen hundred years before the Christian era. This opinion is founded on the events of those times, as they are recorded in the Bible, and we feel fully assured that it will receive the devout consideration it is entitled to receive from every well-constituted mind. The sneers of infidelity we totally ignore and despise as the very lowest and meanest thing in the world—the bias, above all others, that degrades human nature most. It makes little, or, indeed, no difference, whether the hapless votaries of such opinions entertain them with respect to historical facts or doctrinal points; the cruel evil of their scepticism is the same. But to return to our theme. Canaan was at the period alluded to severely suffering from a seven years' famine, which drove Jacob and his household to Egypt to their long sojourn in that country. Five hundred years thereafter, or twelve hundred years before Christ, we read that intestine war raged in Canaan. At that date we venture to fix the period at which the last migration of the Celtic tribes took place, and under the leadership of Gaal, of the line of Hamor, king of Shechem, when, as pretender, trying to regain the kingdom of his ancestors. (See Judges, ix. 26–41.) Having been overpowered in an unequal combat by the men of Abimelech, it is natural to suppose that Gaal would for ever quit his fatherland, and with his men follow in the track of his predecessors from Canaan to seek his fortune in the West until he found them in the peninsula. It is equally natural that his countrymen would there and then readily recognise his royal lineage, elect him their chief, and name the country of their adoption after him. His name distinctly adds credence to this opinion. The variation in spelling between Gaal and Gaul is easily settled. According to the unpointed reading of the Hebrew, it should be Gol or Gaul, and not Gaal, which is the pointed system. This fact also strengthens our opinion. We mention, moreover, that the affinity of Gaelic to Hebrew is apparent only when the latter is read without the aid of the Masoretic points,—a fact, as we observed above, which of itself destroys the integrity of that system. Let me remark here, that Gol may be the origin of *Colla*, a man's name very common among Highlanders. It has come down by the tide of tradition that the first settlers of Caledonia came from Spain. It is even recorded that " *Colla ccud-chathach Spaintcach*—that is, Spanish Coll of the hundred conquests,—was the ancestor of the MacDonalds, Lords of the Isles.

The Celts must have moved westward from Græcia at a period at least three hundred years before Homer's time, under the name of κιλται and Celtæ, according to Greek and Roman historians, to allow a sufficient space of time for the Greek tongue to become moulded into the noble form in which it appears in his book. We may gather this from the analogy of our own English, and the time it took to be collected together, and become moulded into the form it wore at the era of Shakspeare. Homer wrote his Iliad, or sewed together the war ballads of his time, when Solomon, king of Israel, wrote his Proverbs. Chronology makes them contemporaries. Their respective languages, in the productions they have left to the world, stand out in the luxuriant beauty of their genius. By that period the Celtic tribes would have been in possession of the provinces of the West, in which they were found, for several centuries ere they could become so formidable a body as Julius Cæsar found them. Long before his day Britain was wholly peopled by them. It is not a few years, nor even a few centuries, it required to cover the entire British islands with inhabitants, and these inhabitants a Gaelic-speaking race. They labelled the country from shore to shore in Celtic topography and nomenclature. During the Roman invasion and occupation of these islands—some four hundred and seventy or five hundred years —their language, the Latin, made no sensible impression towards changing the local and territorial names. To this day, in North Britain especially, every mountain range and valley, strath, stream, headland, bay, island, and loch, with their Abers, Achs,

Bens, Blairs, Cars, Croms, Dals, Duns, Druims, &c., &c., are purely Celtic descriptive names, thoroughly intelligible to any Gaelic scholar. We do not know how far back it is that these names were given to the country. They are transmitted by the chartularies and other national monumental records; but the most valued channel of any is the vernacular speech of the country, which still survives the dreary past in its tones and accents as a living spoken tongue, without any material change, conveying down to our times these names in their purity and integrity. Let those who admire the English tongue so much, which, in comparison with the Gaelic, is but the mere patch-work of yesterday, be not astonished at us in these parts for our zeal for the integrity of our venerable language, what it still is, and what it was for the last three thousand years. We repeat, that no material change, we can detect, has come over it in all its peregrinations during that period in Scythia, Græcia, Latium, Gaul, Britain, Ireland, and Caledonia. The Welsh, the Manx, the Irish, and the Caledonian Gaelic are the same stock, branches of the same family Celtic tree. We cannot help concluding that Caledonia, from never being conquered, and so never overrun by other tribes, retained the purest branch of it.

Whatever satisfaction may be derived from this result now come to by our investigation—and we trust that, without any exaggeration, our position is well fortified by argument and illustration—the point arrived at which pleases ourselves most is the one which resuscitates the Hebrew vowel-sounds by the aid of the Gaelic, the last surviving daughter of that venerable mother of all languages. The audible living tones of that living tongue, whether echoed from the romantic glens of Caledonia, the green straths of Erin, or the metalliferous ridges of Wales, are the same, and reverberate the same, through the mountains of Judah, to awaken from her long slumbers that revered old parent, to let us once more hear, in her own solemn tones, the promise as Abraham received it, and the Law of God as Moses rehearsed it off the tables in the ears of Israel. The result thus arrived at, we repeat, is no ordinary satisfaction to us, and the claims of our language to consideration are obvious. It is still spoken by, or preached to, above half a million of loyal subjects throughout the Highlands, and yet it stands unrecognised in any of our universities. In this respect we of Scotland are as yet in shameful contrast with Ireland, where they have so many Celtic Professorships, and even behind England and Wales. Aspirants to the clerical profession in the Highlands, if they speak Gaelic indifferently, cannot help themselves. The cause of their inefficiency is a national neglect, which Lords and Commons should acknowledge as such, and speedily remedy.

It is no small grievance to witness the public appearances of those defective in the language, putting out their best efforts, and yet sadly mangling the fair proportions of the beautiful Gaelic into comic shapes and odd sounds, more calculated to upset the gravity of the audience than to edify them.

It will not be out of place here to remark, that throughout the entire Highlands, should there be in a congregation but one solitary hearer that does not understand Gaelic, for that one hearer an English sermon is got up and preached. Throughout the entire Low Country, where the English or Scotch is the spoken tongue, not a word of Gaelic is preached (except in a few cases in large towns), even in parishes which are yearly frequented by crowds of Gaelic-speaking people from the Highlands going to the labour market, who cannot appreciate, if at all understand, an English discourse. We simply allow the two cases to stand in contrast. A great grievance it doubtless is to our poor Highlanders; but the fault does not entirely lie with the Low Country clergy. If the Gaelic were a compulsory branch when they were at college, they would have learned, and be proficient in it, but it is not even a voluntary branch at any of our universities. It is a defect in the national system of the university education of our land. There is, moreover, a defect in our ecclesiastical system, which does not require of all candidates for the ministry, before taking orders, to be qualified to edify their hearers in the spoken languages—*only two* —of the realms. When we send our sons out to become mercantile men, they require, of course, now-a-days to learn French, and other continental tongues, for transacting business; they must go and attend French masters where they can be had. Those who prefer the Church as a profession, I would like to know what excuse they can urge for not using similar means for perfecting themselves in the necessary requirements of their sacred calling. The claim should not be hung up until private benevolence steps in to its relief. It is a national grievance, that calls for national interference to speedily relieve it. The other learned professions, no less than the Church, require to be versed in the spoken languages of the country. The lawyer is not fit to support all the points of the case he conducts without knowing the language in which his client is best understood. It would be absurd to expect that a medical practitioner is able properly to catch the type of the malady of his patient, whose language, in describing the symptoms, he cannot understand. Clearly, then, all lawyers, including pleaders and judges, all doctors, and all the clergy, should, as a requirement of their profession, be properly versed in the two spoken languages of the country. The study of it, we assure them, is not beneath the dignity of their professional calling. Let them but reflect that Queen Victoria's children, and the children of the nobles of the land, think it not derogatory to their high station to sit down to acquire it. Literary men, including professors, divines, critics, newspaper editors, and newspaper contributors (though last, not least) need not affect to give the cold shoulder to the language which lies very much at the root of all their classic lore, and to which these classics owe, as we have just seen, so much of their beauty and literary richness. However, if they choose rather to continue consistent in venting out on our famous old language their usual sage encomiums, as an "antiquated," "useless," and "ready-to-die-out jargon," they may burn incense at the shrine of these old idols—let them do it ; but, in doing it, we must tell them that their cherished employment is simply the perpetuation of their own ignorance. Where, in all the extent of human history, is it known that the study of languages ever interfered with social progress ? Yet there is not in our day a more favourite theory than, Do away with the Gaelic before you can improve the Highlands ! This slang is the doctrine of only shallow and selfish adventurers. It is so fragile in texture as really cannot bear an overhauling ; we pass over it in pity and contempt. Did their native tongue ever hinder Highlanders in the height to which they rose as scholars, as colonists, as scientific men, and as soldiers ? Until they can answer all these and similar questions by logic and grammar, we leave the sapient theorists and their dupes to their cogitations, assuring ourselves that the Gaelic language will not die out while Hebrew, Greek, and Latin are written and known, while the Gael or his descendant inhabits any part of the globe, or while dwells in Highland hearts the native chivalry of " *Tir nam beann, na'n gleann, 's na'n gaisgeach.*

PRINTED BY NEILL AND COMPANY, EDINBURGH.

ON THE

ANTIQUITY OF THE GAELIC LANGUAGE

SHOWING THE IDENTITY OF THE

PRESENT VERNACULAR OF THE HIGHLANDS

WITH THE

GAELIC OF ANCIENT TIMES.

A Supplementary Essay.

BY THE REV. D. M'INTYRE,

MINISTER OF KINCARDINE, ROSS-SHIRE.

EDINBURGH:

WILLIAM P. NIMMO.

1866.

EDINBURGH :
PRINTED BY SCHENCK AND M'FARLANE,
ST JAMES' SQUARE.

PREFACE.

———◆———

THE following Paper is intended as a sequel of the Essay on
the same subject, published by me last year. The proof of
identity of the ancient and modern Gaelic which is adduced,
is meant to show, not indeed the whole that can be said, but
only a sample of the universality of that proof. It is much
to be regretted that prejudice, whatever gave rise to it against
the Gael and his language, has stood in the way of this species
of study being prosecuted more than it has been by the historians of this country, which sufficiently accounts for the
poor and meagre contents of their chapters of our early
history. Had they been capable, by erudition, of conducting
an impartial inquiry into the Celtic topography, nomenclature, religion, and poetry of ancient Alban, it would have
tended materially to assist them doing justice to the social
condition of its early inhabitants. It would likewise have
prevented occasional bursts of gratuitous obloquy, indulged in
by certain writers, devoid alike of good taste and truth, in
dealing with the Caledonian nationality and character. To
point in the direction of that desideratum, is the object of the
following Supplementary Essay.

D. M'INTYRE.

KINCARDINE MANSE, ROSS-SHIRE,
   March 1866.

IDENTITY OF THE GAELIC OF ANCIENT TIMES

PRESENT VERNACULAR OF THE HIGHLANDS.

———————

HAVING last year published an Essay on the antiquity of the Gaelic language, showing its intimate connection with Hebrew, Greek, and Latin, it will be proper, as a sequel of that Essay, to show, and it is the object of this paper to exhibit, the identity of the language of Gaul and Caledonia in ancient times, with that spoken and written by the present Highlanders.

The changes which take place from time to time in the idiom and construction of a language, are chiefly owing to the invasions made upon its territory by tribes speaking different tongues, and by committing to writing their mixed medium of intercourse—formed by incorporating together the speeches of the promiscuous community. Languages, like the tribes speaking them, do not necessarily alter in character or condition if left alone—unassociated with the elements of change. A speech may enrich itself by multiplying vocables, increasing affixes for enlarging its significancy, without making any alteration in its idiom and general construction. Nature around us is our assurance that this opinion is correct. For the proof of it, let us only look at the natural forests that adorn our mountain scenery, and the grasses and flowers which deck the dell, and we see no foreign intruder there, unless introduced by mechanical means ; but the same indigenous tenantry, running out their perpetual lease of the crags, and the valleys, and the plains, without change of appearance, any more than in the tones of the chirping songsters that flitter among them. We have the fact established, that a language of itself does not change, in the history of the early inhabitants of the plains of Shinar, when they betook themselves to the daring project of building Babel, a fort, as they thought, of everlasting strength. The first confusion in their speech was the result of a miracle, while every succeeding change of dialects or languages is the operation of human means. Not until that miraculous fiat at once mixed the speech of that colony had their language any chance of change, that we read of. We may hence conclude that the Gaelic of Caledonia continued quite entire without any alteration, having received into its code no foreign element, just as the gallant and noble race, who spoke it as their language, maintained their independence through the fortunes of so many centuries. Their language, like themselves, repelled foreign intrusion.

It may be satisfactory, however, that this point should rest on other undoubted proof besides reasonable deduction. It will in that case be necessary that we throw a glance into such ancient records as furnish to us, by the direct assertions of their authors, the object we desiderate. In doing so, requires that we once more commence in the East, and work our way westward, following the probable track of the Κελτοι from upper Canaan to Gaul and Britain, and we will in all likelihood detect our object in the following course :—

    I. In the nomenclature of the Κελτοι or Celts.
    II. In the topography of their countries.
    III. In their religion.
    IV. And in their poetry.

In discussing these four points, it may be necessary that the I. and II. should be bracketed together, and the III. and IV.; because the respective subjects of each couplet are so intertwined into each other, as to render it scarcely practicable to be managed otherwise. The nomenclature and topography, mutually interwoven, are subservient of our object; and so are the religion and poetry of our Celtic ancestors.

(I. and II.) That the Κελτοι or Celtæ—speaking the Gaelic, which we still perfectly well understand—were the first great tribe which migrated from the East to Europe, no one nowadays will have the hardihood to doubt. As a clear and undoubted evidence of this, I have shown in the former Essay how largely the Celtic language enters into the foundation of the Greek and Latin, as well as the strong 'resemblance' it borrows from the Hebrew, the venerable mother of all languages. We trace many instances of Celtic topography in the far East, with the nomenclature of the tribes that were its inhabitants. It was about as early as the history of man that he gave his own name to the land he inherited. That early established practice is still continued by the nobility of Great Britain—so with many of the commoners. In the names of Eastern tribes, rivers, and mountains, we have traces of pure Gaelic, as is now spoken at our firesides in Caledonia, without alloy or mixture except what the Hebrew supplies. A sample is all that can be reasonably expected in a paper of this compass. Accordingly, we have in the following nouns, as we shall see on being explained, Gaelic as pure as at this day spoken in any township in Lochaber. Take as an example:—

	Araxas	Ararat	Armenia	Scythia	Pelasgi
Gaelic,	Arachas	Ar-athar-ait	Ar-bheinnean	Saighteaich	Pel-aisigaich

And is thus fully explained. In Ararat, Araxes, and Armenia, the *ar* is Hebrew, signifying a river. Then *ar-athar-ait* is the sky-high-mountain of the river. Araxas is a rapid river of Armenia, hence its name. *Arachas*, that is *ar*, the Hebrew for river, and *chas*, the Gaelic for rapid. Here we are to observe that the *x* is aspirated, and has the force of *ch* hard, as the Spaniards pronounce it in Texas and Mexico; they make it, not as we do, but *Techas* and *Mechico*. This shows that the Spanish language, and, indeed, the French, borrows a large element from the Gaelic, which some, who may be ignorant of Gaelic, think that the mixing element is borrowed from the Latin. Then, Armenia may mean *ard-bheinnean*, *athar-bheinnean*, or *ar-bheinnean*; that is, the high mountains, sky-mountains, or the mountains of the river *ar*. Scythia and Pelasgi mean *Saighteach* and *Pel-aisigaich*; that is, bowmen and ferrymen: the former because they handled the bow and arrow, the latter for having made some progress in navigation, and *ferried* themselves from the East to Peloponesis, to Greece, and to Italy. *Pel* means people; and *pobul* is made up of *bo* and *pel*, or *bul*, which means cowherds; hence any company of persons met together, as in a congregation.

Still farther, let us trace the meaning of the following names, all of Gaelic origin, viz.:—

	Greece	Italy	Alps
Gaelic,	Greig or Greigh	Eadailt	Ailp
	Latium	Pyrenees	Appenines
Gaelic,	Leathad	Bear-bheannan	Ap-bheaunan

Whereof the explanation follows. *Greig* or *greigh*, a flock, from the number of islands, like a flock, which dot the Grecian sea; and also from the fineness of the climate and grazing, so suitable for the rearing of flock and herds. *Eadailt* is evidently from *feudail*, herds, as the early produce of that fine country. *Ailp* means high, while *leathad* means low-lying. *Bear-bheannan* means mountains with scallopy outlines, sufficiently characteristic of the Pyrenees, and *ap-bheannan* means simply high mountains.

In connection with this let us now state names of tribes who had a share, in no small degree, in making up the early list of the settlers of Europe, and shall only give the

Celtæ	Umbri	Teutoni	Sarmatæ	Sclavia	Scand*
Gaelic, Gaeil	Aom-bruich	Tua-dhaoine	Scirm-aitich	Scal-vich	Sgian-dich

These are all easily reducible to Gaelic origin, describing the occasion which gave its rise to each. *Gael* is said to come from *geal*, fair skinned and fair haired, which was characteristic of the Celts of Gaul. *Aom-bruich*, declivity, because they occupied the high ground of Italy; hence the British word *bury* is a corruption of our Gaelic *bruich* or *bruach*, a hill-side town, hence any town; and when they were joined by the Pelasgi of Greece, they took the name of *leathadich*, Latium, that is, low-ground men. *Tua-dhaoine*, Teutoni, because they invaded Germany from the north. *Scirm-aitich*, sonorous-voiced men, and *Scal-vich*, scurling-voiced men, may, with strong probability, be ascribed as their name to these barbarous tribes, who came from Asiatic Tartary. *Sgian-dich* may denote either the wing-like shield or the knife-like weapon which these Scandia carried as their armour. All these names were given them from a Celtic point of view. I will not attempt to reconcile with a Gaelic origin some of the names which succeeding tribes, in their mixed condition, got or assumed. If they have any Celtic element, it is so eclipsed in the barbarous gibberish of the Tartaric savages as to become unknown. For instance, the *Angli* and *Saxons*, descendants of the Sarmatæ and Sclavæ, who can attempt to give a Celtic etymon? Or who can reconcile the Gaelic itself with the Sclavonic, with its thirteen vowels?

In tracing the Gaelic from the East to Britain, it were worse than idle to try to gather up the smashed and obtruncated fragments of it which lie strewed among the modern languages of northern Europe, or even among the high or low Dutch. Such an attempt betrays at once the disingenuousness of the adventurer who tries to do it, to deceive both himself and his readers. There is a path I pointed out in my former Essay which, if we steadily keep, shall guide us to our object. That path is from Minor Asia to Greece, from Greece to Latium, from Latium to Gaul, and from that to Britain. To wander far either to the right or left is sure to land us in a mist of difficulty. It is only those who know not the subject that, as a rear-cover for their ignorance, pretend to be

/censorious in this matter. They affect to state, without a
et / single proof to ~~rebut~~ their statement, that Celtic antiquities,
/ in order to be properly traced, should be guided by means of
the modern scholarship of Germany! Who ever heard of so
preposterous a doctrine? We readily accord to the modern
German scholar the full merit of his achievements, but certainly not to dabble into Celtic antiquities until he first
chooses to sit down and become a perfect Gaelic scholar.
(*See* Campbell's "Language, Poetry, and Music of the Highland Clans," p. 19).

Examples have already been adduced of Celtic topography
and nomenclature in Gaul, and we now proceed from Gaul to
Britain. We must premise by observing, before we leave the
peninsula for the West, that Italy received its first settlers
from the ancient Celts, known by the name of Umbri, a corruption of *Aom-bruich*, as has been explained above. This is
attested by Roman authority of great note, which would be
unjust for a moment to call in question.

> Umbrorum gens antiquissimus Italiæ existimatur.
> *Plin.*, lib. iii.

> Umbri antiquissimus Italiæ populus.
> *Flor.*, lib. i.

When the Gael came first to Gaul, and from Gaul to our
island, is a prehistoric event that is shrouded in impenetrable
darkness. That the brave race pushed their westward, as
well as their northward, way from the far East, is abundantly
attested on the authority of Livy, the celebrated historian.
He denominates them "ferox natio" in the following passage:—

> Ferox natio Gallorum pervagata bello prope orbem terrarum.
> *Liv.*, lib., xxxviii.

That these brave people colonised Britain and Ireland is
vouched by Diodorus Siculus.

> Ferocitate excellent Galli qui ad arctum remote, sicut Britanni a qui-
> bus Iris (Hibernia) habitatur.
> *Diod.*, sic. v.

In opposition to this, to say that some other tribe occupied
Britain previous to the Gael is what we shall not venture,
even though the venerable Bede, a Saxon monk who wrote in
the beginning of the eighth century, asserts it. (See various
other errors of Bede's exposed in Robertson's "Proof of the
Gael of Alban," pp. 125-130.) The utmost we feel inclined to
accede, and which any reasonable mind can ask, is to leave
that point in the meantime an open question. In absence of
any historic evidence, we are bound to go on probabilities,
and that should lead us reasonably to conclude that the hardy,

heroic Celtic race, who with colonies overspread Europe—at
least as far north as the Baltic—earlier than any other race,
would also send a colony, as its first settlers, across to Britain;
they could so clearly espy it from Gaul, and so conveniently
make a descent upon its shores in their *currachs*. It will be
proper here to notice the etymology of

	Britain	Alban	Caledonia	Ireland
Gaelic,	Breatuinn	Albin	Gael-nan-dùn	Erinn

which are thus explained. *Breatuinn*, that is *brait-inn*, high
island, in comparison with the flats of Germany and Gaul,
from which it was espied. For a similar reason *Albinn* was
given it for its high mountains. Those who think they trace
the name to the Latin adjective *albus*, white, labour under a
strange mistake, not considering that our country received
these titles, in all probability, ere the Latin was yet moulded
into a language, and ages before a stone was laid in the foundation of Rome. *Gael-nan-dùn*, that is, the Gaels of the hills,
or *Coille-dhaoine*, wood men, according to Colonel Robertson
in his "Proofs of the Gael," will sufficiently account for the
Celtic meaning of Caledonia. *Eirinn* means *iar-innis*, the
island to west, as we shall hereafter more fully explain.

It will not be necessary to our purpose to enter farther
into a statement of the different migrations from Gaul to
Britain, or the various names by which the tribes were known
who planted themselves to the south of the Tweed and into
Wales. The Cimbri and Belgæ merged into the general name
of British; and, uniting with them the Silures, make up to us
the origin of the Welsh of our day. Any one who takes the
trouble to examine, will find that fully two-thirds of the
Welsh language, as at present written and spoken, is Gaelic,
written in phonetic orthography, and the remainder ancient
British and other foreign vocables. In passing we observe
the Celtic of

	Cimbri	Belgæ	Siluris
Gaelic,	Giom-bruich	Ballaich	Silùrich

To arrive at the meaning of these,—*Giom-bruich* is a compound of *giom* or *giomanach*, a hunter, a gilly, hence a free-
booter; and *bruich* hillside, or hillside hunters or freebooters.
Ballaich or *balgaich* means parti-coloured, from their peculiar
dress, the tartan of their time, and may also mean that the
Belgæ were a mixed race. *Silùrich* is too obvious to require
a lengthened explanation; it is *sil-ur*, a new race, or tribe
that came over from the Continent, and, united with the other
inhabitants, constituting the ancestors of the Welsh nation.

Having thus reconciled with a Celtic origin the nomenclature of the principal tribes who immigrated into this island, at a period too early for the cognisance of written history, we will proceed to examine its topography, in so many instances as may be necessary for establishing the point before us, namely, the antiquity of the Gaelic language and the identity of it, in these early times, with our present vernacular. It would be the height of absurdity to ignore that obvious truth. All the words we have analysed are as plain to any Gaelic scholar as his own name; and why should any one, knowing that fact, hesitate to avow it? It is due to the ancient language itself, and due to our brave Caledonian ancestors who spoke it, and also to their bards, whose sublime productions form the theme of admiration of every unbiassed mind. The interest of this subject will vastly increase upon us as we come now to examine the Celtic topography of Britain. It will not be necessary for us, with a view to this, to rake together *all* the instances of it that come within our reach,—a few of the leading names will serve our purpose equally well as if we gathered up the entire catalogue.

	England	Scotland	Wales	Ireland
Gaelic,	Sassun	Albain	Gimbra	Eirin
	Maun	London	Liverpool	Bristol
Gaelic,	Mannuin	Lod-dùn	Linne-laithid	Cathair-shodoir
	Swansea,	Carmarthen	Kent	Cromar
Gaelic,	Albertamhi	Cathair-mhartain	Ceannt	Cromaird
	Durham	Berwick	Thames	Tweed
Gaelic,	Duneilm	Bear-nig	Tamhain	Tua-aid
	Tees	Esk	Severn	Clyde
Gaelic	Deas	Uisge	Seimh-bhurn	Cluaidh
	Tay	Dee	Don	Edinburgh
Gaelic,	Tabha	Dian	Domhain	Dun-monaidh
	Glasgow	Dumbarton	Fife	Malvern
Gaelic,	Glas-chu	Baille-chluaidh	Ros-mhuc	Maol-bhearn
	Grampions	Argyll	Ayr	Selma
Gaelic,	Garb-bheannan	Ear-ghaeil	Inner-àir	'Seall'ma'
	Cona	Lorn	Morven	Bennevis
Gaelic,	Comhan	Latharn	Moroirn	Beinn-nimhais
	Bencruachan	Glendually		
Gaelic,	Cruachan-beann	Gleann-duali		

It will require considerable space to submit a short explanation of all this list.

Sassun is uniformly the Gaelic name for England, meaning, of course, Saxon. *Gimbra* is Wales.

Albain is as uniformly the name for Scotland, and no other name whatever, meaning high island.

Eirin means *iar-innis*, the island to west. Whether in Latin, Greek, or English, the different modifications of the word are clearly traceable to *iar-innis*, contracted *Erin*. How it got that name may be interesting in the absence of any historical record to submit. We cannot help thinking that our supposition will be found feasible, though grounded on probability. What we are to submit, goes far to prove that Ireland got its first inhabitants, as well as its name, from Alban, as is vouched by ancient historians. The Milisian system, as it was called, is, we believe, nigh given up. Then, what we are to submit is this, that Ireland got its name, the only name it ever had, *Erin*, either from the standing ground of the ancient Celts on the Mull of Galloway, or the Mull of Kintyre: we think the latter. On their progress westward, whether overland or coastways, makes little difference; when they came to the point of Kintyre, they found it *ceann-tìre*, or end of the mainland, as the word implies. From that point, looking southward, they had two islands in their eye, one of them lying to east, *car-innis*, which is Arran; the other to the west, *iar-innis*, which is *Erin*, or Ireland. Any impartial reader cannot resist the obvious force of this supposition, grounded so well on these descriptive names, and carrying so strong a probability of truth along with it. On their farther progress to the west side of the promontory, the early colonists would next see the island of Isla, in the Gaelic *ìle* or *ì-eile*, another island, which they naturally so name, the same way as Lochiel means *loch-eile*, another loch, or an extension of *Loch-linne*. Still farther on, the Island of Mull would be espied in the distance, presenting a mound-like appearance, hence its name, *Maol* or *Mulla*, Mull.

Mannuin is the Gaelic for the Isle of Mann, meaning Monkland.

Lunnain is the common Gaelic name for London, which comes from *lod-dùn*, or *lon-dùn*, that is, the fort of the dib (river-pool), or the fort of the fen — sufficiently descriptive, either name.

Liverpool.—The Gaelic is *linne-laithid*, that is, the pool of the slush, or the low-lying pool, which is sufficiently appropriate.

Bristol is *cathair-shodoir*, the seat of St Saviour, or Sodor, from the Greek σωτηρ, a saviour. σωτηρ is a compound word, though Grecians may not think it such, of the two Gaelic roots *saod* and *fear; saodfhear*, in its original bearing, means saviour, or one who rectifies what is wrong or out of order.

Swansea, *Abertamhi*, that is, the outlet of the still stream. *Aber* is Gaelic, *i.e., cabar*, a miry place.

Caermarthen is obviously *cathair-mhartain*, the chief seat of St Martin.

Kent is *ceannt* or *ceann*, the headland of the country south of the Thames.

Cromar is *crom-aird*, the round headland or promontory.

Durham, *dùn-cilm*, the fortress of the palm. Dunelm is still the Episcopic title of the bishop of that see, which is a farther authentication of the name.

Berwick is *bear-ùig*, the scallopy creek, from some remarkable appearance in the natural outline of the place. *Abertuaid*, i. e., Tweedmouth, is another name for Berwick; in like manner, the Gaelic name for Wick, in Caithness, is *inner-ùig*, and for Thurso, *inner-corsa*. Inver, i.e., *ion-ar*, good soil; *cluan* is another name for it.

Thames we make *tamh-amhnin*, still river.

Tweed, *tuathaid*, that is the river that flows to north, hence Tweeddale is *dail-thuathaid*.

Tees, *Deas*, the river to south.

Esk, *Uisge*, water emphatically.

Severn, *scimh-bhurn*, smooth water.

Clyde, *cluaidh*, the winding river, as *cluanan* means the winding banks of such a river, hence rich green pasture.

Tay, Dee, and Don, mean respectively *tabha, dian, domhain*, i.e., still river, rapid river, and deep river.

Edinburgh is *dun-monaidh*, the hill fortress, was its earliest name, thereafter *Dun-eidin*.

Glasgow is either *glas-chu*, gray-hound, named after a famous Fingalian deer-hound; or, according to other authorities, *glas-ghobha*, the gray smith, a celebrated maker of swords in these early times.

Dumbarton, anciently *al-cluich* and *bal-cluich*, either of which means the town of Clyde; *dun-bretuin* is its present Gaelic name. The origin of *bail* may be *aile* or *aileachd*, with the formative *b*, an impression, as a town is the impression of an inhabited country. Or *baile*, a town, may come from *ba*, cows, and *fàl*, a divot enclosure; *ba-fhàl* and *bo-fhàl*, contracted *baile* and *buaile*, a fold, hence a town. We have, on the authority of Virgil, that in early times the houses in Italy, as in the Highlands, were covered in with divot.

Pauperis et tuguri congestum cespite culmen.
    Virg., Ecl. i.

This clears up the difficulty raised by some of reconciling with a Gaelic origin the name *Al-cluch*, the town of Clyde, or Dumbarton. We may observe, in passing, that *town* or *toon* is a British corruption of *dùn*, a fortress; so the somewhat modern name Dumbarton, is *dùn breton*, or town of the Bretons. They err who think they make out what they call a British or Cimbric element in our topography, in the *abers*, *invers, tons, pits, llans, tres, coms, cims,* or *cums,* etc., etc., which by proper analysis are all Gaelic.

Fife took that name from Fifus Duffus; so Cambden; but the original Gaelic name was *Ross-mhuc,* the promontory of the swine, doubtless the wild-boars which were so keenly hunted by the Caledonians. The chief town, St Andrews, was originally called, after the promontory, *ross-mhuc,* and more recently *Cill-riobhin.* Hence Culross and Kinross, *cul-ross* and *ceann-ross* mean, respectively, the back and head of the promontory.

Malvern means *maol-bhcarn,* that is, the round hill with a scallop in the outline.

Grampions, *garbh-bheannan,* rough mountains.

Argyll, *Ear-ghael,* the tail of the Gael country. This particularly alludes to the promontory of Kintyre, which, like the tail of a fish, runs so far out into the Irish sea.

Ayr takes as its Gaelic name *inner-àir,* the inver of the river called the *àir.*

Selma is *scall'ma'* for *scalladh-math,* a good view, which Selma certainly commands. It lies in the parish of Ardchattan, Argyleshire, and was, in its day, headquarters of Fingal and his Feinian heroes. The spot bears the name of Beregonium, from what origin we know not.

Cona is *comhan,* the river Coe, that run through the glen of that name.

Lorn, *lathearn* or *laighearn,* is supposed to be the same with Lora of Fingalian fame, and means land of calves—not a misnomer by any means.

Morven and Morvern, *mor-bheinn* and *mor-earran,* that is, great mountain, and great bounds; either spelling is fully significant of the scenery.

Bennevis, *beinn-nimh-bhathais,* that is, the mountain of the cold brow, from the perpetual snow it keeps.

Ben-cruachan, by transposition, becomes in Gaelic *cruachan-beann,* and means the cone-shaped mountain.

Glendually, by late geographers, gets the ridiculous spelling of *Glendoili.* The Gaelic spelling, from which the English is derived, is *gleann-dubh-lighe,* the glen of the black water, a very appropriate name. In this way many names throughout the Highlands are seriously damaged by the ignorance or carelessness of geographical writers. In this instance, the error will not be allowed to pass uncorrected; the glen in question being our birthplace; with its towering mountains, most romantic corries, charming forests, and rich grassy slopes, to which the sympathies of our boyhood are closely bound. Besides, it furnishes a remarkable relic of the Fingalian times, in *tom-na-cloiche-finne,* that is, the knoll of the Fingalian monolith. A huge block of stone, of enormous weight and size, stands on the summit of that knoll, which he who traces these lines could see every day he looked out, as an object of strange familiarity. The same sightly knoll supplies a name to the adjacent lofty mountain, and ravine, and corrie, as *beinn-an-tuim, cas-an-tuim, coir-an-tuim.*

We submit that list of names as a mere specimen of Celtic topography and nomenclature peculiar to the British Isles in early times. No available authority can produce, or condescend on, any earlier topography respecting England or Scotland. If so, and it is not too much to assert it affirmatively, without fear of contradiction, no people could have preceded the Celts, who left behind them those indelible traces of the tongue they spoke in the land of their adoption. We would speak advisedly, but do positively and unhesitatingly affirm, that this point defies contradiction. The prestige which the Celts possessed at the era of the Roman invasion, is another evidence of the same truth, by the high head they carried as a great and very formidable nation. The Romans, during the four hundred and seventy-five years they occupied South Britain, were obliged to construct walls to protect themselves against the incursions of this bold and daring enemy, who met these Roman invaders in many a fierce engagement, and stood their ground unbeaten and unsubdued in their Caledonian mountain fastnesses. That they were formidable rivals, we have on respectable Roman and Grecian authority.

Murum . . . . duxit qui Barbaros Romanosque divideret.
Spart. in Hadriano, xi.

Μεγιστος δε ὁ Βρεττανικος, etc., etc.
Dio. Cass., lib. lxxii.

The bravery and prowess of the Caledonians were sufficiently tested in meeting the well-trained Roman legions, which is doubtless referred to in the poems of Ossian. Localities are mentioned, still identified by the same name as the banks of the winding Carron (a small river in Stirlingshire), and the sounding Cona (the river of Glencoe in Argyllshire), which were familiarly known to the Fingalians, and known by the same name in our times.

Upon the whole, then, we feel confident that, in the foregoing analysis, we have shown the identity of the ancient with the modern Gaelic, which is as obvious to any Gaelic scholar as the letters of the Gaelic alphabet. In the full belief of this, we now proceed to show still farther the evidences of it as are furnished by the religion and poetry of the Gael in ancient times, which forms the

(III. and IV.) Third and fourth sections of our Essay, and which shall be discussed in combination, rather than separately.

The truth is, it would not be so practicable to adopt any other method. The poetry of the Caledonians is not in that respect different from the poetic productions of other nations, but embraces the religious and moral code, along with the exploits of the people who were its heroes.

In proceeding with this section, it is my bounden duty to acknowledge how deeply indebted I feel to the interesting and able productions of two authors of works on kindred subjects; and I frankly own how little the occasion is of writing this Paper, considering the superior merit of theirs, had not one of these authors himself suggested the task to me. One of them lives east, the other west, of the Grampions—both retired army officers; who, after nobly serving their king and country, for a long period of years (*See* Campbell's "Language, Poetry, and Music of the Highland Clans," p. 41), now, with their swords hung in the hall, take up the pen of the learned and wield it well, as a still farther service to their country. I allude to Colonel James A. Robertson, author of "Historical Proof of the Gael of Alban;" and to Captain Donald Campbell, author of "The Language, Poetry, and Music of the Highland Clans," both works recently published, and of rare merit. As very monoliths, they convey to remote posterity the fame of their authors, in letters far more indelible, than by any Parian obelisk. From a home point of view, nothing can be finer than to see the *amor Patriæ*, which so fondly dictates such a task to retired army officers, who devote the afternoon hours of their useful lives to the clearing off the dust of prejudice, and the mist of obscurity, overlying the early pages of their country's history. They thereby show, from undoubted evidence, the social refinement of their early Caledonian ancestors. This latter act is the happy counterpart of their former doings; their literary labours reflect lustre on their military achievements. In both phases we easily recognise the leal-spirited Gael; and such, in truth, they are —descended of illustrious Highland families,—one of them a claimant of the Breadalbane peerage and estates.

To return to the archives of the past, we find it testified on good authority that Polytheism was not known to the ancient Celts. This of itself is, by the way, a farther evidence that the Greeks and Romans, and consequently their language, could not precede the Gael and the Gaelic. In the midst of the Caledonian forest, or traversing the sea in their *currachs*, the Gael owned but one God, the Lord of the Universe—a fact which assigns to themselves and their language an early Eastern origin. This is vouched, in respect of the Celts, on the following authority:—

Celtæ colunt quidem Deum.
Max. Tyr. Dissert. xxxviii.

Regnator omnium Deus.
Tacit. de mor Germ. xxxix.

Unum Deum fulguris affectorum, Dominus hujus universi solum
agnoscunt.   *Procop. Goth.*, lib. iii.

It is thus abundantly evident that the Celts owned but one
Deity when the Greeks increased the catalogue of theirs, to
keep pace with their abstracted notions, till at last the number of their gods were about thirty thousand. Accordingly
the Δις of the Greeks, and the Θεος, with the oblique cases of
Ζευς; the *Dis, Ditis,* and *Deus* of the Romans are manifestly
derived from the *Dè, Di, Dia,* and *Ti* of the Celts; and, as
Mr James M'Pherson rightly observes, the only name by
which the Deity is known to those who speak the Gaelic of
Alban and Ireland. In the Gaelic *E* signifies he, and, by pre-
fixing the formative *d*, becomes *De* or *Dia*—literally, *the Being*,
emphatically, God. The Druids worshipped one God, in their
"clachans" or stone circles, seen to this day, notwithstanding
the positive assertion to the contrary of several ancient
writers. The old Gauls were said to worship three divinities,
under the appellations of *Teutates, Hesus, Taranis.* So says
Lucan, in his Book I., as follows :—

Et quibus immitis placatur sanguine diro
Teutates, horrensque feris altaribus *Hesus*
Et *Taranis* Scythiæ non mitior ara Dianæ.

These, however, seem to be three names of the same Being,
rather than three separate intelligencies, which is clear by
submitting the words to a legitimate analysis. Then the
three words Teutates, Hesus, Taranis, divested of their Latin
terminations, become *Teutat, Hes, Taran*—easily reconciled with
Celtic origin. Teutat is just *De-tat,* the God that is; *Hes,*
the Being emphatically, and *Taran,* thunderer. The great
Goddess Diana of the Grecians is nothing else than a borrowed
name, derived from the Gaelic *Dia;* and, by Grecian abstrac-
tion and Polytheism, conceived to be a feminine divinity. It
is hence obvious how easily we can realise the identity of the
old Gaelic with our own vernacular. This is evident, also,
by tracing to a purely Celtic origin the names of the most
conspicuous heavenly bodies, which opens the way for us to
look into our ancient Gaelic poetry, where such terms are of
frequent occurrence. Accordingly, Grian, the sun, is from
cri-theine, the quivering fire, from the dazzling effect its rays
have upon the eye that looks at it. *Grian* is the same word
in Ossian's Poems of the third century that it is in our

mouths of this present age, without change or modification of any sort. It is doubtless the origin of the *Grynæi* of Virgil—

Ilis tibi Grynæi nemoris dicatur origo
Ne quis sit lucus, quo se plus jactet Apollo.

Virg. Ecl. vi.

According to Strabo, Apollo, the God of the sun, had a temple in the Grynean grove, built of white marble, where was a famous oracle; and in no grove did he glory more, as Virgil has it in the above lines. This is an instance in which the vagaries of Polytheism are traced up to a common origin; and, by the help of our vernacular, we can arrive at that origin. *Aise* is a sun blink, and by the formative, *d* or *t* becomes *taise*, a ghost, and is no doubt the origin of Αισοι and Αεσαρ, which, according to Seutonius, were Grecian deities. *Taise* the Celts of Gaul were said to regard as a spirit, and so the name still, which acted on matter; and *De*, the Supreme Divinity, or soul of all material substances. *Luan*, which means full, is the early Celtic name for the moon; hence *luna*, the Latin name. *Diluan* is Monday, or moon's-day. *Rè* is another name for the moon; hence *reul*, a star, is from *re-cile*, that is, another moon. And so on, other words in endless variety, which form the only good criterion we have of preserving inviolate the proper pronunciation of Greek and Latin tongues. The Gaelic is the only living language which pre-existed and which survives them, unchanged and inviolate. It would be an insult to common sense not to concede to it, and to it alone, the safe custody and preservation of the vowel sounds and intonations of the dormant Hebrew, Greek, and Latin. This is asserted in our Essay of last year, and now, after more mature deliberation, more emphatically repeated, that in this matter the Scotch schools have the decided preeminence over those to the south of the Tweed. Though the English ear may find it more harmonising with their own peculiar taste to adopt what is called *their* pronunciation of the classics, we hesitate not to tell them, on the testimony of antiquity and of the Gaelic language, that they are simply *wrong* in their entire experiment of needless, useless, capricious vocalisation.

The paradise of the Celts of Britain was called *flath-innis*, that is, the island of nobles or of heroes. Than that there is to this day no other name in the Gaelic tongue for the state of the blessed. It was the language of Ossian, and it is ours . without any change. The only change is in the locality of the *flath-innis*. The light of the Gospel has happily shown to us, who live under it, that our *flath-innis* is not, as our ancestors conceived it was, an island in the western sea, begirt with storms and tempests, for warding off impious intruders; but, far away in the heaven of heavens, guarded and begirt in everlasting peace, with never-ending calm. The Gaelic has no name for hell, as such, except the idea of an island with constant rain, *ifrin*, that is, *i-bhuirn*. There is extant a very glowing description, by certain Latin writers, of the island of the blessed, or *flath-innis*, which it is not necessary to give here at length.

Celebratæ illæ beatorum insulæ dicuntur esse occidentali oceano.
Eustath. ad Dion. Perieg.

The Celts of Caledonia had their *bards* and *seannachis*, that is, poets and chronologers; the Irish Scots their *fear-dans* and *fear-laois*, that is, songsters and hymnists, who sang the praises of their warriors and great men.

Bardi quidem fortia virorum facta . . . . cantitarunt.
Amm. Marcel., lib. **v.**

This brings at once before our mind the office of the Fingalian bards, which any one who peruses their productions will easily realise; but before submitting quotations we shall offer a few remarks on the dress and dwellings of our Celtic ancestors.

The ancient Celtic over-dress was the "*sagum*" of Gaul, or *ság*, which is the Scottish plaid; hence *sáigean*, *ságach*, derivatives of *sag*, meaning the clogged muffled-in appearance which the wearer of it presents. The *braccæ* is the *breachdan*, from *breac*, spotted or parti-coloured. *Feillidh*, the Highland kilt, is derived from *fillidh*, a fold, and *breachan-an-fheillidh*, plaid of the kilt, formed the Highland full-dress—a continuation of the kilt folded over the shoulders and round the waist, which altogether took twelve yards of tartan fabric for its ample dimensions, and not the ridiculous apology of the *brachdan-an-fheillidh*, that is nowadays wore. We have, on the authority of Tacitus (*de Mor. Germ.* xxii.), that the Celts were very cleanly in their habits. They bathed regularly every day, while the Sarmatæ of Asiatic Tartary were filthy to a proverb. From the Celtic dress, accordingly, we trace the identity of the ancient and modern Gaelic. Let us now observe as to the Celtic dwelling. They did not live in towns. Their *baile*, or homestead, was a clump of trees, where they had their hut, surrounded by a fence or foss to secure them against accident by fire. We have shown above the origin of *baile*, and may observe here that the πολις of the Greeks is derived from it, and their καλυβη, a covering, from the Gaelic *callaid*, a covering, or division of a house. That this was the Celtic mode of living is testified.

20

ου πόλεις εχουσιν...εν χαλυβαις διαιτωσι.
Dio. Cass., lib. **xxxix.**

Oppidum Britanni vocant, quum silvas impeditas vallo atque fossa
muniverunt.   *Cæsar*, lib. v.

Having traced up the identity of our Gaelic as spoken nowadays with respect to the Celtic homestead, we pass on to
look into the Caledonian poetry, as compared with the Gaelic
poetry of our own times. The poems of Ossian take of course
the first place among the Celtic records of antiquity. It does
not now seem necessary to us that any argument should be
advanced bearing on their authenticity. Time has vastly
added to the proof of it. Any scholar who can peruse these
sublime productions in the full meaning of the Gaelic original,
his intellect cannot possibly be so obtuse as not to appreciate
them. The internal evidence of authenticity they carry is
overpowering. If any deficiency existed in their external
evidence, it is supplied by the publication of the book of the
Dean of Lesmore, which was written, as the date of it bears,
between the years 1512 and 1529, or about two centuries
before M'Pherson was born. Those who so fiercely opposed
Ossian's magnificent lays, what would they now say if they
were to look up and see Dean M'Gregor's manuscript?
Verba scripta manent tells equally against them in the lucubrations they have committed to writing, and in favour of
Ossian.   Dr Johnson and his copyists grounded their objec-
tions upon *no manuscript;* but since an objection any how
seemed their aim, they might, even with a manuscript, with
the same facility transfer that objection from *no manuscript* to
no authenticity. Ossian's Poems, in the hands of any just
critic, will be allowed, like Homer, Virgil, and Horace, to speak
for their own authenticity by their burning words, without
the manuscript over which the authors consumed the mid-
night oil. We know just as little, or as much, of the manuscripts of the latter as of the former; transcripts are all that
we have of each, and quite sufficient. The Poems of Ossian
have already *lived down,* and will *outlive,* the fame of all their
traducers. The course of time, and the force of sound induc-
tion and literary progress, have fully exploded the Johnsonian
objection, whether urged by himself in his not very philoso-
phic or courteous style, or by the cuckoo notes of a shallow
troop of servile admirers. The crusty lexicographer left
London for the Highlands, it is true, fully primed with Saxon
prejudice against everything Scotch or Highland, except, as
fell from himself, the high road which led back to London.
And not all the Scotch kindness and hospitality that were
heaped upon the man by the Boswells, Burnetts, M'Leods,

M'Leans, etc., etc., could divest him of that prejudice. To that bias alone can we attribute the stern bearing of the learned Saxon, whose inward nature could be touched on the fields of Marathon and among the ruins of Iona, and yet stood inexorable over the sublime pages of Ossian. The splendour of the Ossianic couplets, rich in the choicest imagery, and conceived in cultivated taste and pure morality, all glowing in bright poetic fire, had no impression on the Sarmatæan spirit of Johnson. To show the transcendent descriptive powers of the Fingalian bard, let us quote a passage from his Address to the Sun, and if there be any poetic composition outside the Sacred Record finer, in any ancient or modern author, all we say is we never yet met it.

> O! thusa fein a shiubhlas shuas
> Cruinn mar làn-scia-chruai' nan triath
> Cai as a tha do dhearsa gun ghruaim
> Do sholas a ta buan, a Ghrian!

No translation, however literal or however free, can possibly catch the poetic grandeur of these lines, or of the entire poem. The rhythmic harmony which balances every line and every couplet, whose every sound is the echo of the sense, is a very needless effort to try to convey by any translation. For the convenience of those who do not understand Gaelic, it will be as well to attempt as natural a rendering as we can of each line as they stand:—

> O! thou thyself that glides above,
> Circular as the full-orbed shield of steel of the brave;
> Wherefrom is thy blaze un-bedimmed—
> Thy light everlasting—O, Sun!

Our purpose in giving the quotation is purely to show the identity of the Ossianic with the present Gaelic of the Highlands. The grammatical accuracy of it and its phraseology are the same. There is not a word or syllable, or allusion or figure, but is perfectly plain to the comprehension of any Gaelic scholar of the nineteenth century. It is not only the same Gaelic, but the same identical dialect of it. To assert otherwise would be open rebellion against truth and propriety. Let us not, however, affirm so strongly on the merit of a single passage, but quote a few lines from some other poem of Ossian; let us take the beginning of *Carraig-thura*, on the Setting Sun, and we submit that the glowing description is simply inimitable.

> An d' fhag thu gorm-aster nan speur,
> A mhic gun bheud a's òr-bhui ciabh.
> Tha dorsa na h-oiche dhuit fein,
> Agus pailliun do chlos 'san iar.

Thig na stuaidh mu'n cuairt gu mall,
A choimhead fir a's glaine gruaidh ;
A togail fo eagal an ceann,
Ri d' fhaicinn cho àillidh 'na d' shuain.
Theich iadsa gun tuar o d' thaobh.
Gabhsa cadal ann do chòs,
A Grian !

To throw it into natural English it runs—line by line,—

Hast thou left the azure course of the skies?
O guileless son! of the yellowest golden locks.
To the portals of night thou betakest thyself;
And to the tabernacle of thy repose in the West.
The billows shall slowly roll around,
To behold him of the most shining cheek ;
With awe raising aloft their heads,
To espy thee so charming in thy sleep.
They fled colourless from thy side.
Enjoy thou thy slumbers in thy cave,
O Sun !

In the same poem, farther on, is a passage describing the encounter of Fingal with the Spirit of Loda, which serves the double purpose of showing that the Fingalians were not idolators nor a timid credulous race, and that their language and phraseology was the same as nowadays in the Highlands. No poet ever invested his hero with bravery of the same intrepid type as that which Ossian attributes to Fingal—of meeting in single combat alone, under the cloud of night, the terrible spirit of Loda, the presiding deity of the Scandinavians. The majestic grandeur of the passage is undescribable, except in the ornate poetic polish of the original. Fingal is exhibited to us, with his glittering sword unsheathed and raised aloft as he majestically advances to meet the frightful spirit, of huge mountain size, with loud, dreadful menaces, which the brave King of Morven despised, and met in threats not less severe, as follows:—

Thog Fionnghal san oich' a shleagh
Chualas anns a' mhagh a ghairm
" A mhic na h-oiche o mo thaobh
Gabh a ghaoth agus bi falbh
C' uim thigeadh tu m' fhianuis fhir fhaoin
Do shambladh cho baoth ri d' airm

*   *   *   *

As m' fhianuis a dhubh-mhic nan speur
Gairm d' osag dhuit fain 's bi falbh !"

To which the dismal spirit replied—

" Teich gu d' thir fein a mhic Chumhail
No fairich gu dubhach m' fhearg !"

Dhaom è gu borb a chcann ard
Ghabh Fionnghal na aghaidh le colg
A chlaidheamh glau gorm 'na laimh

*   *   *   *   *

Ghluais solas na cruaidhe ro' 'n taibhs'
Fuathas dona bhais fo ghruaim
Thuit esa gun chruth 's è thall
Air gaoth nan dubh charn ; mar smùid.

The elegant translation of M'Pherson conveys the meaning
of this sublime passage very well indeed—as much so as a
translation can do it; but we prefer, as in the above extracts,
to give the natural rendering, line by line:—

> Fingal wielded aloft his sword in night,
> His shout was heard aloud in the high expanse.
> "Son of the night, away from my borders,
> Take the wind and begone.
> Why comest thou to my presence, thou shadow?
> Thy form as unreal as thine arms.
> From my presence! gloomy son of the clouds,
> Call thy breeze to thyself, and begone."
> "Fly to thy own land, son of Cumhal! ⎫
> Or feel, to thy sorrow, my wrath!" ⎭ said the spirit.
> He bent boldly forward his lofty head.
> Fingal advanced to the combat with heroic air,
> With his blue gleaming sword in his hand ;
> The gleam of his steel cut through the ghost,
> With the grim terror of death in the blow ;
> The ghost rolled over, shapeless in its fall,
> On the wind of the dark mountains ; like smoke.

The coherence can easily be traced in every line, which is
managed with the exquisite skill of the bard, by compressing
without crowding, so much poetic thought into his highly-
finished couplets. It bears comparison, and even excels, the
most perfect production of the Muse in ancient or modern
times. Any one who can read and appreciate the one cannot
fail to appreciate the other. The idiom of the Gaelic of
Ossian—simple and eminently comprehensive, though of an
exquisitely transcendent strain—is as obvious as the phraseology employed by "Duncan Ban M'Intyre," or "Mac Mhais-
ter Alister." But some will perhaps be inclined to say that
certain of the old Gaelic manuscripts to which Mr James
M'Pherson, the elegant translator of Ossian's Poems, had
access, were written in a different type and style from what
we nowadays understand,—such, for example, as the manuscript of the Dean of Lesmore, which was written in the
character and style of its day, between the years 1512 and
1529. Let us see what such an objection contains, should any
one think of starting it. The better way will be to give a

specimen from that interesting manuscript, which is as follows :—

> Derrymir wlli gi dane,
> Ach Finn ne waene agus Gowle,
> Dethow churrych fa hard keym ;
> Wa na reym skoltyt ny downe.
> Ne yarnyt tam na tocht,
> Gir yoyve calle si phort ynaa ;
> Ych techt doy her in ness,
> Derre ass maccayve mnaa.

This is Gaelic doubtless, but it is written in phonetic orthography, savouring, as we must admit it strongly does, of the Gaelic of Ireland. This is not to be wondered at, considering the attending circumstances. The Dalriadic colony which came over from Ireland to Argyleshire in the year 506, incorporated their dialect with the speech of that county, along with the intercommunion between the two countries, which from that period to this day exists, with the possible certainty that Dean M'Gregor knew the Irish better than the Caledonian Gaelic, will sufficiently account for the character and style of his book. The consequence is that the Dalriadic, or, at any rate, visible traces of it, are to this day found to pervade the Gaelic of Kintyre, Arran, Bute, Cowal, Islay, and Lorn, as far up as Lesmore, where the Dean penned his manuscript. The Gaelic in this quotation is, with that exception, as pure as any other, though at first sight it wears a somewhat strange and unsightly dress,—a garb equally foreign to it, as if you were to see a Gael rigged out in knee-breeches and Scotch cassock. The metamorphosis did not, however, change his nature or his language ; he speaks his vernacular as fluently as in his kilt and hose. The Gaelic should regularly be written in its own proper orthography, so as to preserve its native tone and accent. It is quite as unnatural to it to be clothed in such a habit as the above, as it is for the Cockney, or other southron anti-Celtic guiser, who decks himself out in the borrowed feathers of the Highland dress. We maintain that those who are not Highlanders, or who affect to despise the beautiful language of the Gael, have no right whatever to assume his elegant dress. The noble costume should never be seen thus smuggled and degraded in decorating the externals of any incongruous interior.

Let us now exhibit the above passage in its natural orthography, which is thus :—

> Dh' eireamur uile gu dian,
> Ach Fionn nam Feinn agus Goll ;
> D' fheitheamh a churaich fo ard cheum,
> Bha na raimh ag sgolt' nan tonn ;

Nior dheanta tamh na tochd,
Gur ghabh cala sa phort ghnu ;
Ach teach doibh thar an cas,
Dh' cirich as macamh mna.

Of which the English rendering is as follows. It is not ours :—

We all rose up in haste,
Except Fingal of the Feinni and Gaul ;
To wait on the high-bounding vessel,
Which in its course was parting the waves ;
It neither slackened nor rested,
Till it entered the wonted haven ;
But when it sailed over the fall,
There rose out of it a beautiful woman.

We deem it unnecessary to add anything to what has been submitted to prove the identity of our Caledonian Gaelic—the Gaelic of the Fingalians in the third century, and that of the Dean of Lesmore twelve hundred years later; and we are not without specimens of the same kind during the intermediate space. There is ample proof in the transactions of the Highland Society of other Gaelic MSS. existing, to which Mr James M'Pherson had access, when taking down and translating Ossian's Poems. Considering Mr M'Pherson's temperament, his high sense of honour, and how his fidelity was impugned by the aspersions of incompetent and ungenerous critics, on the question of the existence of a MS., it is not at all to be wondered at, that he would not stoop to submit those in his possession to the equivocal scrutiny of disingenuous eyes. He knew well that the sublime lays of Ossian would clear a way for themselves, despite the ignoble surmises thrown out against him and them. Among those who imbibed the virulence of Johnson, appears a Mr Shaw, who published what he calls "Remarks on Ossian's Poetry;" being the result of a journey he made to the Highlands and islands in spring 1778; for he, too, was ambitious of authorship, in the department which gained laurels to M'Pherson. Any one who peruses the lucubrations of this writer will feel no astonishment from his unbecoming remarks at his ill-success in gaining the confidence of the Highland clergy, or others possessing Gaelic MSS. He, and all others who floated along in the same tide of opposition, have, by uncalled-for virulence, left on record such materials of their own condemnation as cannot now or hereafter be perused without intense pain. It is, nowadays, discreditable to the feelings and intelligence of any scholar who can read, without appreciating, Ossian in the original, or in M'Pherson's elegant translation. Such then is Ossian, our Alban Homer, his country our country, his Gaelic our Gaelic.

We flatter ourselves that this is made out in this Paper, now brought to a close, by the topography,[1] nomenclature,[2] religion,[3] and poetry of our Caledonian ancestors. We submit it without fear to the discriminating eye of an impartial public, well assured that the facts produced are such in good faith, and that no contrary facts are available to upset them.

[1] Modern writers, unacquainted with the Gaelic language, are liable to be mistaken in the derivation they give to local and territorial names on the sea-coast of the north of Scotland, fancying that they are dealing with Norse originals, while in reality they have Gaelic roots—rounded, indeed, and rather disfigured, by the effort of Norse accentuation. It is not a little singular that archæologians and antiquarians should not bestow on the rightful origin the benefit of originality. They may perhaps think it more fashionably learned to do otherwise; but we submit, that to reach the rightful source by a logical, legitimate path, that no one can gainsay, is preferable.

[2] It is in accordance with the above note that mistakes in nomenclature are often committed. An egregious instance is, how they hand over to the Norsemen the ancestry of Somerled, Lord of the Isles and Thane of Argyll. Would not the simple fact undeceive them, that he was all his days the great enemy of the Norsemen? Those who cannot pronounce a word right, should not for that reason give it a wrong origin. So far from being Scandinavian, Somerled, as they called him, owned a long line of Caledonian ancestors: "Somhairle Mòr Macgillebhride," whose grandfather was Gilledomnan, descended of "Colla ceud-chathach-Spainteach." Any one with the smallest pretensions to Celtic tradition knows that.

[3] The simplicity of the religious ideas of our Caledonian ancestors, without the presence of Polytheism, claims for them an Eastern origin. Those who love to deal in the marvellous may take a full swing in what they call the "Aryan theory of languages," and we wish them joy of their aerial dream. Sober thought can scarcely give place to the supposition that an obscure tribe, living to the north-west of India, could be the linguistic repository of all our early European tongues, including the Celtic, of course. If they mean the Sanscrit as the chief member of the Aryan, let them not overlook the strong points of affinity, or rather identity, between it and the Greek, which dooms the former to a comparatively modern origin. The structure of the verb, so similar in Sanscrit and Greek, with a middle voice common to both, is ample evidence that they were originally cast in the same mould, and long posterior to the Celtic, which furnishes a large element in their groundwork.

www.ingramcontent.com/pod-product-compliance
Lightning Source LLC
Chambersburg PA
CBHW021552270326
41931CB00009B/1176